When the Sickness is Over...

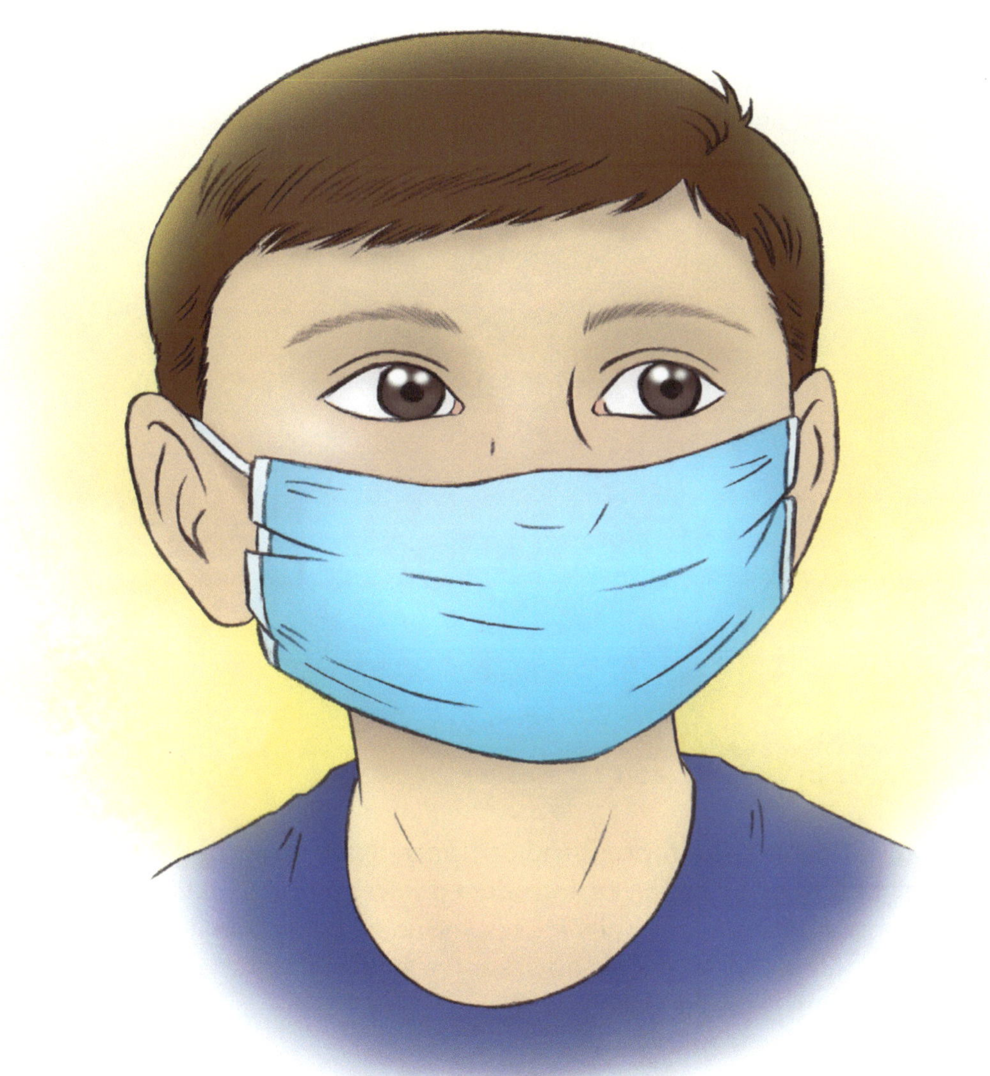

Lee Johnston

DORRANCE
PUBLISHING CO
EST. 1920
PITTSBURGH, PENNSYLVANIA 15238

Dorrance Publishing Co
585 Alpha Drive
Suite 103
Pittsburgh, PA 15238
Visit our website at *www.dorrancebookstore.com*

ISBN: 979-8-88925-993-0
eISBN: 978-1-6491-3538-4

When the Sickness is Over…

When the sickness is over…

We can go to the playground again, but we have to
wear our masks

And wash our hands when we get home.

When the sickness is over....

We can have play dates again

As long as my friends wear their masks too.

And we still need to wash our hands after we play.

BOO

When the sickness is over….

We can go visit Grandma and Grandpa again.

I really miss them and I'm glad they are okay.

And when I get home, I will wash my hands really well.

When the sickness is over…

We can do a lot of things again,

But I need to always wash my hands and use my mask.

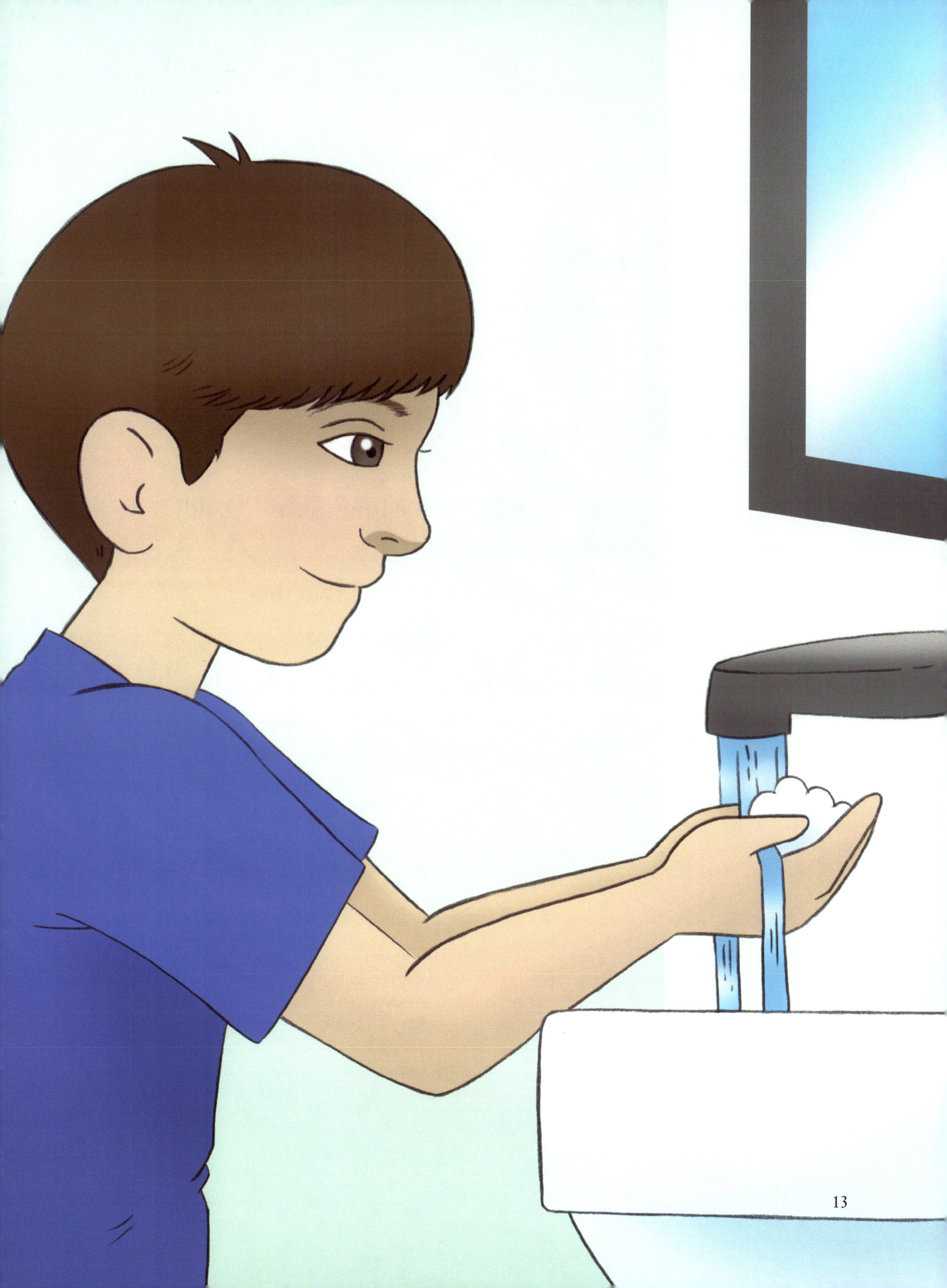

I like to ride my bike with Mommy and Daddy.

We ride around the block together.

We always wear our masks and
wash our hands when we get back home.

If we go to school in person

We wear our masks!

I love seeing my friends and my Teacher
in my classroom

When I have school online

I don't have to wear my mask

I sit at my little table and use Mama's computer

I try my best to listen and do my work

I see lots of people and kids wearing masks

That's different now and it's okay with me,

Because when the sickness is over

We will all be okay.

The End